Dedication:

Volume 3 Project Space:
600 Mission St. SE, Salem, OR 97302

The Dedication Project

1

Dedication:

Volume 3 Project Space:
600 Mission St. SE, Salem, OR 97302

The Dedication Project

Authors:
Lois Stark
Sandra Schaefer
Doshiell House
Baby Bear
Cynthia Herron

Created by: Arianna Warner

For all the people who dare to be different.

I admire your courage and freedom to be who you are. You are a lighthouse to the rest of us who long to fly with our fresh wings. Stay strong and clear about your mission. We need you!

For my Mother..

My mother has given everything- her time, money, energy, and well-being to put me where I am today. Without her eternal help and guidance, I would have been stuck in a small town with no prospects. Her sacrifice has given me my life, my identity. Thank you, Mom! I am a stronger, smarter, and more informed of a woman because of you. Despite the years of living off of emergency food supplies, we've made it to a real life. Thank you, Momma. Now it's my turn to take care of you.

For everyone who ever gave a chance, who believed and went out on a limb.

Dedicated to the soul seekers, artists, and dreamers who understand that we're all in this thing called life as one and want to help each other out. Praise God, but I dedicate this to my Mother for always saying and doing positive things. I love you forever!

For Papa.

Because of the stories and the music and the noise and the names. Because of the circle that won't be broken.

For Jay.

He walked over to the wild plum grove with me this morning. Our lab-mix Lucy watched us... it was already hot and we were hoping the small green plums were riper than the last time we walked past. I stopped under a drooping bough and right away saw a golden green plum, soft and ripe. When I looked over to see if he had found any, I saw he was holding an entire branch down so he could reach the ripe fruit at the top. He picked one, then bit one end off and ate it. Then he took the pit out with his teeth. With his free hand, he lowered the rest of the ripe plum to Lucy. He has taught me again and again about kindness and generosity.

For

Intentionally left blank for others to dedicate.

11

For

13

For

15

For

Intentionally left blank for others to dedicate.

Dedication Index

Acknowledgments

Special thanks to all the authors and those who participated in Volume 3: Project Space 600 Mission St. SE, Salem, OR 97302. Thank you to the Salem Art Association for the opportunity have The Dedication Project be apart of Project Space 2014.

Thank you Kathryn Cellerini-Moore for your mentoring, friendship, and support. Rawr!